PIAOTT Publishing & Graphic Design LLC.

God's Design: The Prerequisites For Becoming A Successful
Intercessor
Gail L. Hurt
ISBN: 979-8-9892562-5-9
Copyright © 2023

DEDICATION

I cannot express enough thanks to my Father God in Heaven for His continued love, support, and encouragement, the grace and favor He has placed over my life, and for the opportunity to be used to help encourage, be a steppingstone, help others become all God has created them to be in the earth.

I would like to thank my sister Lynn Carter for all the prayers, and encouragement and for being my biggest cheerleader. My mother Martha Carter for all her prayers love and support. I also want to thank my son Jayden Myles for being my motivation.

TABLE OF CONTENTS

GOD'S DESIGN

The Prerequisites For
Becoming A Successful Intercessor

GAIL L. HURT

PREFACE

You will never forget the day the Lord spoke over you that you were an Intercessor! You were excited for several reasons. You now know the direction God is taking you, and it has brought you more clarity in what God has called you to and what He has called you to operate in. When you get the word from the Lord, you just wanted to dive right in! But, when you did, you discovered resistance, backlash, and Spiritual Warfare.

God wanted me to share with you that it is a process to becoming a great Intercessor. The cleansing (Deliverance), relationships (Development), and the tools for Intercessors (Deployment) must be embraced, connected, and latched on to so that you can become the successful Intercessor God has called you to be.

Heart of Worship

When I think of the body of Christ, I think of an

actual body. I believe that each church or person in every state operates as a certain part of the body. For example, one church or person might be the head while another church or person is the legs, etc. We all need each other, and when one part of the body is wounded, it affects the other body parts.

The Midwest, where I come from, lies at the heart center of the United States (Nebraska.) God has trusted me to the main part of the body, the heart! The human heart is an Organ that pumps blood throughout the body via the circulatory system, supplying oxygen and nutrients to the tissues and removing carbon dioxide and other waste. Without the heart, the brain cells can only survive 4 minutes without oxygen, and then the brain cells start dying! If there is no heartbeat, the heart is not contracting, the blood is not circulating through the body, and there is no oxygen supply.

So, let us look at this as if this is the body of Christ. God has given everyone the ability to help pump blood throughout the body, supply oxygen and nutrients, and remove carbon dioxide and waste. We are helping the other parts of the body to be able to function by doing our jobs. God is a God of order. Think about the human body; everything is in order! That is why it is important for Kingdom connections, and I pray this book will be able to link with other churches or persons in the Midwest to work together to help get the body of Christ back to its original state. And because God has trusted us to maintain the important part of the body, which is the heart, we must also maintain our own hearts. My heart desires to leave no man behind!

I will never forget all the times I gave up on church because I did not understand what was being said or taught. I have had a learning disability since I was a child. I stuttered badly, my comprehension was low, and my reading was horrible. I always had to go to a Special Education class or group to get one-on-one teaching. As I got older, in junior high and high school, I began to rebel. There was a lot of skipping school to the point of dropping out because I felt like I could not keep up with everyone else. So, I ran!

When I gave my life to the Lord twelve years ago, I began to have those same feelings of running because I could not understand all the big words being used and a lot of the teachings I could not understand. And to top it off, I was a babe in Christ just beginning my journey. I was too embarrassed to raise my hand in bible study to ask if someone could break down what was being taught or even ask what certain words meant, so I stayed in the back and kept quiet. I would even buy all these different books on Intercession to enhance what God has placed on the inside of me. Still, the books would be so big and thick with all these big words, so I spent a lot of time googling every other word in the book, and for someone who has a reading problem, it becomes frustrating!

I received a prophecy from someone stating that I would write a children's book. I tell you what, I looked to the left and the right, then back to the woman of God like she missed it! First, mams (Chuckling), I do not like anything that looks or sounds like schoolwork, and two, I don't even deal with children like that! As I grew in the Lord, that planted seed began to form. I suddenly had this desire to write a book on Intercession for beginners in Christ or anyone who has suffered the way I did.

My heart does not want anyone left behind! If I could write something plain and simple in English terms, straight to the point, to help catapult them to their next place in God, that's what I'm going to do. So, this book is not for the experienced. It is simply for Beginners in Christ or Intercession. I pray this book will give clarity, direction and bless your next level of Intercession.

God Bless!

Ezekiel 22:30 says....

"I looked for someone among them who would build up the wall and stand before me in the gap on behalf of the land so I would not have to destroy it but found no one. And it goes on to say.... So, I will pour my wrath on them and consume them with my fiery anger, bringing down on their heads all they have done, declares the Sovereign Lord."

CHAPTER 1

DELIVERANCE
Spiritual Malnutrition

"For the gifts and callings of God are without repentance. They can never be withdrawn."

Romans 11:29

Matthew 15:22,26 says... "And behold, a woman of Canaan came from that region and cried out to Him, saying, have mercy on me, O Lord, Son of David! My daughter is severely demon-possessed. ... But He answered and said, it is not good to take the children's bread and throw it to the little dogs."

Mark 7:27 says... "Let the children be filled first, for it is not good to take the children's bread and throw it to the little dogs."

In these two verses, Jesus refers to deliverance as the children's bread. These words contain a revelation concerning the importance of deliverance ministry. Deliverance is bread for the children of God. It is part of a spiritual diet from which every believer has a right to partake. When deliverance is not a part of a believer's diet, the result is spiritual malnutrition. Bread is defined as food or sustenance.

Sustenance is a means of support, maintenance, or subsistence; the state of being sustained; something that gives support, endurance, or strength. Christians need bread to endure. Without such, there will be faintness and weakness. The reason many believers are weak and fainting is that they have not received deliverance, which is the children's bread. In the verse, "Let the children be filled first..." the word filled means to be satisfied. Just as the natural appetite cannot be satisfied without bread, the spiritual appetite cannot be satisfied without deliverance.

The church has been trying to bring deliverance to the world while ignoring the words of Jesus: Let the children be filled first. In other words, we cannot bring successful deliverance to the world until we bring it to the church, and we are delivered! **Psalm 104:14-15 says, "He causes the grass to grow for the cattle, vegetation for the service of man, that he may bring forth food from the earth, and wine that makes glad the heart of man, oil to make his face shine and bread which strengthens man's heart."**

Bread strengthens the heart; it makes us strong. Deliverance will certainly improve your health. Every believer needs a refreshing. Preaching and teaching are major parts of feeding the flock, but if deliverance is not included, then the flock is not being properly fed. We cannot treat God's word like a buffet; we choose what we want from it and leave the rest. I encourage you to get with a Leader of your local church that has a Deliverance Ministry that can help you become free in your heart and become more effective in the call of God on your life. **2 Timothy 2:21 says, "Those who cleanse themselves from the latter will be instruments for special purposes, made holy, useful to the Master, and prepared to do any good work."**

Matters of the Heart (Deliverance)

One thing that freezes us from moving forward is our heart. God has scanned my heart, and I failed the test! With all the good I was doing, my heart was still broken, deceitful, full of anger, and wickedness. If we are not careful, we can be doing religious work and still be backslidden in our hearts. We may even feel God's anointing and presence upon our works and prayers, which can become a deception. How? Our works and prayer life can be so good that we never stop to recheck our hearts to see if it is in good standing with God. So, I had to ask myself, does Jesus reside inside me? I do not have any doubt that he uses me, but does he live permanently and continuously here? Am I His?

Sometimes, we need to ask ourselves if this is learned behavior. Am I doing these things because I am supposed to? Or are any of the things I do for God, the church, my ministry, are they from the heart? And if so, which heart are we operating out of, the old or the new heart? There is another word for operating from the old heart: Counterfeit. Counterfeit means made in exact imitation of something valuable or important with the intention to deceive or defraud. Fake.

So how do we worship (serve) God in Spirit and truth when we have a wicked and deceitful heart? **Romans 11:29 says, "For the gifts and callings of God are without repentance. They can never be withdrawn."** I learned something about God. He is the only one who will fire you and let you keep working! Just know that his presence will not be in the room. We must be careful not to be deceived by knowing the genuine presence of God versus gifts.

I hear God saying drop your pride and surrender the old heart! **Revelation 3:15-22 says, "I know your deeds, that you are neither cold nor** hot. I wish you were either one or the other. So, because you are lukewarm, I am about to spit you out of my mouth. You say, I am rich, I have acquired wealth and do not need a thing. But you do not realize that you are wretched, pitiful, poor, blind, and naked. I counsel you to buy from me gold refined in the fire, so you can become rich, and white clothes to wear so you can cover your shameful nakedness, and salve to put on your eyes so you can see. Those whom I love I rebuke and discipline. So be earnest and repent. Here I am! I stand at the door and knock. If anyone hears my voice and opens the door, I will come in and eat with you. And you with me. To the one who is victorious and sat down with my Father on His throne."

Hebrews 4:12-13 says, "For the word of God is alive and active. Sharper than any double-edged sword, it penetrates even to dividing soul and spirit, joints, and marrow, it judges the thoughts and attitudes of the heart. Nothing in all creation is hidden from God's sight.

Everything is uncovered and laid bare before the eyes of Him to whom we must give account." God has given us His word to penetrate the depths of who we are and transform us from the inside out. Surrender!

When you have a car, you must keep up the maintenance on it. If you do not, the car will eventually begin to have trouble, and then it will break down. It's the same thing with your heart. You must do a tune-up throughout this race for God! You are going to have to stop from time to time to get an oil change (rejuvenated), sparkplugs (resuscitated), breaks and starters (restored), etc., to be able to move forward and function. Car accidents happen. Dents, scratches, cracked windows, and being totaled out can occur at any time. The same thing happens with our hearts, and sin is not the only cause. Soul wounds and trauma can be damaging to your foundation. Examples are the death of a loved one, rejection from people, divorce, molestation, and verbal, physical, and emotional abuse. These can affect how we move, operate, and flow throughout our walk with God.

I became bored with praying, intercession, dancing, deliverance ministry, etc, because I felt like I was doing the same thing over and repeatedly! I did not know I was hindering my growth by operating with my old heart. God could not pour new wine into old wine skin. So, I could only go so far. **Luke 5:37-39 says, "And no one puts new wine into old wineskins; or else the new wine will burst the wineskins and be spilled, and the wineskins will be ruined. But new wine must be put into new wineskins, and both are preserved." Jeremiah 17:9 says, "The heart is more deceitful than all else and is desperately sick; who can understand it?"** What kind of heart is this verse talking about? Why is the church in the position now of not realizing we need a new heart? Why do we feel by getting our outward appearance right that, we are getting somewhere with God? It is because man looks on the outside, but God looks within the heart. It is our hearts that God is coming back for, nothing else! The mind does not determine whether you enter the Kingdom of God. We should stay focused on what is inside. When we get the inside to line up with God's word, we will change! God will give us a new heart! And this new heart will manifest on the outer man just as the old heart works from the inside out.

In Jeremiah 17:9, the word deceitful means to mislead by false appearance or statement, to trick.

Remember that this wicked heart not only misleads people, but it also misleads you! Another word for deceitful is unfaithful. An unfaithful heart can never be dedicated to God or will never be able to keep a commitment. Therefore, certain relationships do not last, and there is a lack of integrity in the body of Christ. This heart does not have what it takes to be faithful to God or man and has a willful desire built into its mechanism not to perform what is expected or desired. This heart also cannot be penetrated by the word of God! It will not yield to God. The deceitful heart's nature sends us in the opposite direction of God. So, when this old heart hears the word of God, it sits dormant in the sanctuary. The mind may hear the word, yet the heart remains unchanged.

Jeremiah 17:9 also calls this old heart perverse, corrupt, and severely mortally sick. The word severely means grave, critical, and harsh! It is extreme, intense violence in character and nature. This heart destroys everything it touches. It is a heart that will steal your life away. Since the nature is violent, you cannot correct it. When confronting people with a perverse heart, you can expect rebellion in attitude and conversation.

The verse also says, **"Who can know it, perceive, understand, and be acquainted with his own heart and mind?"** When you look up the word acquainted, the question becomes, Who is familiar enough with his own heart to furnish it with knowledge? Who knows the depths of their heart that he can furnish it with the knowledge that it will take to walk toward God?

Jeremiah 9:7-8 says, "The Lord almighty says, See I will refine and test them, for what else can I do because of the sin of my people? Their tongue is a deadly arrow, it speaks with deceit. With his mouth, each speaks cordially to his neighbor, but in his heart, he sets a trap for him." We try to hide who we are and what we do by covering it up with what we say. But when the wicked heart becomes full and active after being fed iniquity, and the mind has assumed complete control, we will see the depths of this old heart operating to its fullest potential. The words of your mouth will speak from the abundance of what is in your heart.

I did not want to admit privately or publicly that God had been dealing with me about receiving a new heart. My pride became a deception. **Proverbs 16:18 says, "Pride goeth before destruction, and a haughty spirit before a fall."** God has shown me that conducting our lives to look like the untouchables, looking like we have it all together like we are perfect, does not leave a straight path for others to follow. The best route for people is to follow a path already trodden, which becomes a point of true leadership. Since we have already walked the spiritual road, just like a mother or father in the natural realm, we should be willing to share these experiences with our children and other people so that they can learn by example. If no one has shown people how to walk, suffer, and endure, then there is no example of how to stand during the battle. God revealed that when He has set you into a position, but you do not have depth in Him, you can only preach and teach and prophesy from the realm in which you walk. You can only raise a person to the level on which you stand. The depth of your deliverance is the depth of the deliverance you can offer another person.

There also must be a purification in leadership. Leaders must begin to seek God for the new heart so that, by way of example, they can provoke the people to want the new heart. God has put his light within us to shine before the world, not to suppress and hide it from others. He does not want to remove the candlestick from its place. **Revelation 2:5 says, "Remember the height from which you have fallen! Repent and do the things you did at first. If you do not repent, I will**

come to you and remove your lampstand from its place." He is calling us to repent. What a privilege and an honor it is when he calls us out of sin and allows us to become acquainted with Him! It is the biggest miracle that can happen in your life because while having a mind that has been conceived in sin and shaped in iniquity, trained by the world and the enemy to the point that you must come into the world prepared to die an eternal death. God is still able to penetrate it.

God has allowed us to hear the gospel, and at that very moment, in that split second, He penetrates the mind that Satan had trained. He puts His word in our mind so that it tells us to, **"Be not conformed to this world: but be ye transformed by the renewing of your mind, that ye may prove what is that good, and acceptable, and perfect will of God." (Rom. 12:2)**

Transformation takes place when our minds are brought to the understanding that we need God. When we do not renew our minds, we can fall away into the old heart. I have learned that the brain never stops working. It never settles down, nor does it ever shut up! Even when you are sleeping, the brain is in motion. The brain, not the heart, constantly races, moves, talks, plans, and visualizes. Without stopping for a breath, it takes us to where we have been, where we are, and where we are going. It is constantly receiving information at breakneck speeds. Most of the time, the heart cannot, and will not, keep up with the pace of the mind.

We get so busy moving and doing things that we do not consider our hearts. In the natural realm, people will have heart attacks, and the doctor will use a defibrillator to jump-start the heart that has stopped beating. It reminded me of the church. There are so many Christians racing around with spiritual heart problems that we need to be resurrected when we get to church! The choir, preacher, and praise teams must be our spiritual defibrillators. They get powered up and send out an electrical charge into the congregation. They are trying to jump-start the hearts that have stopped beating. The treatment keeps you going for a couple of days, but that heart is still mortally sick. It needs to be replaced.

Here are a few verses the Lord shared with me if you choose not to receive the new heart.

1 John 1:5-6 says, "God is light, and there is no darkness in him at all. So, we are lying if we say we have fellowship with God but go on living in spiritual darkness. We are not living the truth."

1 John: 8-10 says, "If we say we have no sin, we are only fooling ourselves and refusing to accept the truth. But if we confess our sins to him, he is faithful and just to forgive us and to cleanse us from every wrong. If we claim we have not sinned, we are calling God a liar and showing that his word has no place in our hearts."

1 John 2:3-6 says, "When we obey God, we are sure we know Him. But if we claim to know Him and don't obey Him, we are lying, and the truth isn't in our hearts. We truly love God only when we obey him as we should, and then we know we belong to Him. If we say we are His, we must follow the example of Christ."

Let us look at **Songs of Songs 2:15. "Quick catch all the little foxes before they ruin the vineyard of your love, for the grapevines are all in blossom."** It is those little things that we think are not a big deal that will destroy us completely. A harmless lie, cussing, stealing grapes off the vine at the grocery store, backbiting, and anything we put before God. Little Foxes.

My house is nice looking. I get compliments on

it all the time. The one thing people do not know is the foundation is leaning so badly that the doors do not stay closed. If you paid attention, you could feel yourself walking downhill when you walk through the house. Symbolic of how we are on the outside and how we are on the inside. God also shared with me that during this season, I was not to visit other churches, conferences, etc. The reason was because of the heart surgery that was going to take place.

How many of you know that when you are about to undergo a procedure, the doctor will give specific instructions to follow until the due date? Those were my instructions! I did not understand at the time, but I do now. When going through a procedure, only certain people can be in the operating room. Other people in the room besides the team can cause a distraction to all who are in the room. When you are opened, you are exposed! Any and everything can and will try to enter the body and destroy the procedure. God is trying to do a heart procedure, and we are getting up off the surgery table to have others interfere with the procedure. Be still! Trying to get off the table can cause contamination, body parts not being lined up correctly, and the worst part is, now you are walking around with an open wound, bleeding on everybody, causing harm to others because you are now infected.

Luke 11:28 says, "Blessed are those who hear the word of God and obey it."

I encourage you to take a minute and allow God to examine your heart and give you a diagnosis so He can create in you a clean heart and put a new and right spirit within you. Before you move on to the next chapter, take a day or two, maybe a week, and allow the Lord to minister to your heart. And write down what you hear. Also, God is a gentle God. He works in layers. Don't expect everything to be done in one setting. Not only will He reveal, but He will give clear instructions on what, how, and who (if anybody) to begin the Deliverance (surgery) process.

And remember, if you have questions, don't hesitate to ask your leaders for guidance.

NOTES

CHAPTER 2

DEVELOPMENT
Relationship with God

"But the Advocate, the Holy Spirit, whom the Father will send in my name, will teach you all things and will remind you of everything I have said to you."

John 14:26

Colossians 2:7... "Having been firmly rooted and now being built up in Him and established in your faith, just as you were instructed, and overflowing with gratitude."

Colossians 1:10... "So that you will walk in a manner worthy of the Lord, to please Him in all respects, bearing fruit in every good work and increasing in the knowledge of God."

The difference between Intercession and Prayer

True intercession has a far deeper meaning and results from a developed relationship with the Lord that is immeasurable.

Talking to God through prayer is so important. As you develop your prayer life, you come into a deeper relationship. It is words that are spoken from the depths of the soul. It is the most intimate level and creates a bond of trust that is not easily broken. It is the process of becoming one.

Intercession is something else entirely. Out of the depths of prayer, an intercessor is born and developed. It is an act of selflessness and a choice to step into a situation that requires you to come alongside another's battle. In prayer, you are an instrument for God's pleasure. You minister to His heart by giving Him all your heart, mind, soul, and strength, and out of that, oil for the lamp of your life is produced.

When you intercede, you are an instrument for God's purpose on the earth. So, the priority as an Intercessor is to see others come into God's pleasure. The deeper the relationship, the greater God can use you. It is powerful when you feel the love God has for another person. And that is where you pray from instead of your personal feelings about someone. It is transformative. The Intercessor does not allow their inclinations to get in the way of prayer. Instead, the purest flow of God is allowed to travel through them as an oracle to reach the person He is trying to touch (Gateway, portal).

Interceding Changes, the Heart of the Intercessor

The heart of the Intercessor is constantly being conformed to the nature of God because He is sharing so much of Himself and His love for others with you. In every sense of the word, they become more of an imitator of the Father through the constant downloading of wisdom and revelation. Spending more time with God in intercessory prayer makes you more like Him.

Characteristics of an Intercessor (Prophetic)

- Intercessors see through God's eyes, hear as God hears, touch as God touches, taste as God tastes, and smell what God smells. When we can do this, we get the burden of intercessory prayer.

- Intercessors allow God to use them instead of God being used for their benefit when they pray.

- Intercessors can change the mind of God. Moses changed God's mind.

- Intercessors are called to live a disciplined and holy life. God will not hear us if we have sin in our lives.

- Intercessors place a high value on prayer when others don't. You will sometimes get frustrated. Intercessors find it harder to pray when people assign prayer tasks (lists). It keeps you boxed in, not being able to be led by the Holy Spirit. By the time you get to number three on the list, your paper will be on the floor, and you are somewhere else in the realm of the Spirit.

- Intercessors receive revelation from the Holy Spirit on what to pray about and how to pray. Intercessors may be more spontaneous in expressing their prayer gift than others.

- Intercessors have a strong intimacy with the Holy Spirit when they pray.

There are so many other characteristics, but get into discovering what type of Intercessor you are!

Discover your strongest area!

God calls Intercessors into different areas to intercede on behalf of others. Once you find out the area (assignment) God has called you to, the Holy Spirit will begin to help you develop in those areas. I will list a few, but ask the Lord what area he has called you to, and it may be more than one! **Isaiah 11:2 says, "The Spirit of the Lord will rest on him, the Spirit of wisdom and of** understanding, the Spirit of counsel and of might, the Spirit of the knowledge and fear of the Lord."

John 14:26 says, "But the Advocate, the Holy Spirit, whom the Father will send in my name, will teach you all things and will remind you of everything I have said to you."

- Compassion and Mercy Intercessor – Feels compassion for others. Their needs and hurts, sickness, children, people's traumas, etc.

- Transformational Intercessors – Ask the Lord what is needed for a church, city, business, or region to bring change.

- Personal Intercessors – Are called but sometimes appointed to intercede for pastors and leaders.

- Warfare Intercessors – Are involved in high-level spiritual warfare, binding and loosing. They are familiar with demonic and how things work in the spirit realm.

- Birthing or Midwife Intercessors – Birth souls, new ministries, schools, and Godly businesses.

- Worship Intercessors – Access heaven through worship to bring hope to the hopeless.

- Crisis Intercessors – A watchman for God's people. (God can wake you in the middle of the night to pray for someone you may not even know).

Again, it is all about a relationship with God. Where we can be loved completely, challenged to grow in our faith, and transfigured into the exact person he created us to be. Love the Lord your God with all your heart and with all your soul and with all your mind and with all your strength that you may be able to produce and manifest His attributes here on the earth. Being able to operate in any of these requires God to be able to communicate with us and trust us. None of these areas matter if there's no relationship.

I encourage you to take a week or two and press into His presence, meditate on His word, and seek (desire) Him. Ask Him nothing for yourself, make it all about Him, and watch how He will begin to open up things for you, about you and your destiny. Have a pen ready to write. Write down everything you hear, see, taste, touch and smell. Allow your heartbeat to line up and become compatible with His heartbeat so that the same pattern can make a sound (symphony) in the heavens and the earth.

NOTES

NOTES

CHAPTER 3
DEPLOYMENT
Commandments of Intercession

"The LORD is my rock, my fortress and my deliverer; my God is my rock, in whom I take refuge, my shield and the horn of my salvation, my stronghold."
Psalm 18-2

Thou shalt love the Lord thy God with all your heart, soul, and strength. Intercession is not a matter of saying the right words but having the right heart.

Thou shalt not intercede without first hearing from God. When we intercede, we do not inform or persuade God. It is God who persuades us and informs us. We are not putting words in His mouth; He is putting them in ours.

Thou shalt have expectant faith. We should have graduated from a mustard seed of faith to international, world-vision faith. Intercession recognizes no boundaries.

Thou shalt love thy enemies. When we intercede, we take another person's place. This means we can take the place of a murderer, child abuser, etc. To be great intercessors, we must love our enemies, or we will refuse some of our most important intercessory opportunities. Remember, God loves everyone!

Thou shalt expect spiritual warfare. Intercession is so powerful it is a tremendous threat to the devil. An intercessory prayer group is a major offensive against the evil one. We must be ready to fight, rally the troops, and not be foolish enough to go it alone.

If you are willing to be a portal and a gateway for God and follow these commandments, please sign your name on the line.

I _____say yes to your will.

Now that we know what prayer and intercession is about, let us look at how God can use us during intercession.

EXAMPLE: One day, I was picking up my son from school. I had about 30 minutes to kill, so I sat there with my eyes closed. I began to smell something horrible! The smell was so bad I had to get out of my car and start looking for the smell. I looked in the back seat, front seat, and trunk. I said Lord, what is that smell?! And the Lord stated that it was the smell of my people carrying around old dead things. I have slayed the giant in their lives, but they picked up the giant and started carrying it around. I need you to intercede for them to let it go. If they do not let it go, they can go no further; it's dead weight. So, just with a smell, I was put on assignment. When things start to look, taste, smell, sound, or feel crazy, ask God, "What is this?" If you do not hear anything, carry on, but always ask!

EXAMPLE: One morning, I woke up hearing water, could not move my mouth, both of my hands felt restricted, my chest felt like it was caving in, and my feet were kicking. Then, a vision of a woman in a bathtub with her hands tied, a harness over her mouth, her face submerged underwater, and her feet kicking appeared. I shook it off and started praying for the woman, praying that the attacker would be stopped in his tracks! But God said no, no, that is not it. (Remember, I did not ask, so I went all over the moon and did not hit anything). He asked me what did I see and felt and to go look up everything I saw. So, I went to Google and looked up what I saw.

Hands tied – someone is unable to act freely because something prevents it.

Harness – a set of straps and fittings by which a horse or other draft animal is fastened to a cart, plow, etc., and is controlled by its driver.

Head submerged – Force to make someone do

something against their will.

Being held underwater – pressure or persuasion, influence, or intimidation to make someone do something.

Feet kicking – fighting to get free.

God was telling me that I needed to intercede for the saints at that time because they were being controlled (Witchcraft) by the leaders, and people were trying to get free. So, God let me experience what the people were feeling. All five senses were used here. Being an intercessor, you must always stay ready and on your post. When God gave me these assignments, I was not in prayer. He just dropped them on me. You must be ready in season and out of season. Remember, we are a gateway, a portal for God. Our life is not our own anymore. We belong to God.

Targets for Prophetic Intercession
Each area of the church should be covered.

- Pastor (apostle, set man)
- Elders
- Prophets and Prophetic Teams, Intercessors
- Teachers
- Evangelists and Evangelistic Teams
- Help Ministry
- Administrators

- Dance Teams
- Youth Ministry
- Children Ministry
- Finances
- Missions (Nations)
- New Believers
- New Members
- Married Couples
- Single People
- Men and Women
- Widows
- Families

Prophetic intercession also includes prayer for the release of:

- Church growth
- Deliverance
- Evangelism
- Favor
- Gifts of the Holy Spirit
- Glory
- Healing
- Holiness
- Humility
- Love
- Miracles
- Peace
- Prophecy
- Prophetic Worship
- Prosperity
- Protecting Angels
- Revelation
- Salvation
- Signs and wonders
- Strength
- Unity
- Wisdom

When interceding, you should always aim for the target.

When I think of the word target, I think of a Battering Ram. A battering ram is an enforcer gaining entry to premises, gates, and walls. So, we also become battering rams for God. When God gives you something to intercede about, there is always a root to that situation. You must dig deep to get to the root, and once we find it, that is the target. You stay on that target until something breaks or God tells you to let up. You cannot be all over the place when interceding. Some people can intercede for an individual and end up praying for things that do not line up with the target.They get off track and begin to pray for aunts, uncles, grandkids, finances, jobs, etc. Not lining up and remaining on the target is getting into a personal agenda for the person. When part of an Intercessory Team, staying on target keeps everyone on one accord.

EXAMPLE: Last year in August, while the flood in Texas was going on, the leader of the intercessory team wanted to intercede for the victims. As we began, I started to hear the water and could not breathe. The water was brown and dirty, and I could hear the people crying out in their hearts for the mercy of God. As I went deeper, I heard the hearts of some people asking God to forgive them for worshiping idols and doing rituals. There was a lot of child molestation going on. I also saw an underground tunnel where people were doing rituals, and these were people of high power. So, my target was to intercede for the city for the sins that were being committed there, not stopping the water. It was something in God's heart at that date and time that he wanted to focus on the sins that were taking place in Texas. Yes, my mind and heart wanted to pray for the safety of these people, but God had a different agenda. Stepping into the gap and repenting for the sins of these people was saving them.

NOTES

CHAPTER 4
TRAVAILING IN THE SPIRIT
God's Usage Of Us

"Bear ye one another's burdens, and so fulfill the law of Christ."
Galatians 6:2

You can be moved from one place to another, supernaturally. One type of experience is when we are taken in the spirit somewhere, but our physical body remains in the same place.

Most of us do this when we dream. It can also occur when we are awake. Some people travel in the spirit to another location with their physical body, through the dimension of the spirit. Sounds weird, but again I am a witness to this. But before I tell you my experience let us look at some examples in the bible.

Ezekiel was transported in the spirit and describes the experience in Ezekiel 8. He was moved from his dwelling place outside Israel during the captivity and taken some distance to Jerusalem. Paul described his trip to heaven, confessing he did not know if he was there only in the spirit or in his physical body. **(2 Cor. 12:2)** While friends were interceding for Peter, he was mysteriously freed by an angel. It's obvious he didn't know if it was a vision or an experience in the natural **(Acts 12:8-10)** after traveling through a gate, which opened by itself, he arrived at home.

Jesus was often slipping away and reappearing mysteriously. He appeared to the disciples again in a room where the doors were closed, which implies he either walked through a wall or materialized before them. **(John 20:26).** Jesus also made a fascinating comment about the fact that we would do the things he did; **"Most assuredly, I say to you, he who believes in me, the works that I do he will do also; and greater works than these he will do, because I go to My Father. (John 14:12).**

Are you a portal?
A Gateway for God?
THROUGH INTERCESSION SHE IS RISEN

EXAMPLE: I was sleeping, and I found myself in an extremely hot desert-like place. I looked down and saw that I was standing in sand and dirt, the wind was blowing so hard that I could smell and taste, the sand and dirt. I then noticed that I was standing in a hut with something like a torn sheet for the door. I then noticed a family hysterically crying, I walked over to them and asked, "What was wrong?" The mother looked up and said, if I could just talk to her again, hug her again, laugh with her again I would be okay. I walked outside the hut, I looked to my left and saw a big scene, a green jeep and a lot of people crowding around a little girl.

I walked through the crowd stood the limp body up and whispered in her ear something in another language. The little girl began to breathe, everyone was in awe, I took the girl by her hand into the house where the family was, told the family she could be there for a little while, they agreed, they loved her, hugged her, etc. Then I said it was now time, I took the girl by her hand, and she disappeared, the family thanked me, and I woke up.

In this example I traveled far from Omaha Nebraska, my five senses were used, and I also was talking in another language and performed a miracle. I raised the dead! A lot of times when you are interceding in a different location (different region) by the Holy Spirit you can speak in a different language, and let's not forget what the scriptures say; **"He who believes in me, the works that I do he will do also; and greater works than these he will do, because I go to My Father." (John 14:12).** Because God was able to use me to perform this miracle. Remember you can go only as far as your faith takes you! Let us look at a few more ways God can use you to intercede.

Travail

Travail is the posture of desperation. It expresses an urgent prayer of the heart. Travail is the one manifestation of prayer and intercession that is rarely desired, yet which can be one of the most influential and powerful. The expression of Travailing ministers in and affects the spiritual realm. Travail is a God-given expression of spirit-anointed intercession that comes in God's timing and produces the will of God within a given situation in a miraculous way.

Travailing in the Spirit is often extremely hard and can even be quite painful, but what is happening during one's travail is birthing something new through the Spirit. It may be a new job or flow of income, a new ministry or church, or a new season of joy and favor. As an intercessor, you are the lifeline to another; your travail would be to help birth a new thing in their life. The thing being birthed through the Spirit will always be that which God desires.

"Now he who searches the hearts knows what the mind of the Spirit is, because He makes intercession for the

saints according to the will of God." (Romans 8:27)

During Jesus' earthly ministry He travailed heavily for a lost friend at Lazarus' tomb (See John 11:33), and then near the end of His earthly ministry He travailed for the people of the world at Gethsemane Garden (See Luke 22:44.)

Travail is a much-needed manifestation in this season for our generation. In our Intercession, we need the fruit of the Holy Spirit in operation as much as the power of the Holy Spirit. But I believe, if the prayer warriors and intercessors of our day will begin to travail in the Spirit for our world we will see a Christ-driven revival in our land. Now let us look at how you may operate when it comes to burdens.

In Intercession, the Intercessor becomes a carrier of the burden of the Lord. In other words, what is a pain and burden in the heart of God concerning the people becomes a pain and burden in the heart of the intercessor. This burden and pain are generated from deep within the Intercessor's innermost being, which is called in the scriptures "bowels of Jesus Christ" (Philippians 1:8). The main component of the bowels of Jesus Christ in an Intercessor is mercy. Mercy is the foundation of all apostolic Intercessory prayers (Col 3:12). To possess the heart of Jesus whereby we can be touched by the feeling of the infirmities of others, we must have a personal bond with Jesus.

Galatians 6:2, "Bear ye one another's burdens, and so fulfill the law of Christ."

Though all Christians are called to intercede and bear the bowels and burden of Christ, an ordained Intercessor can bear the burden of Christ in a way that no other can. They enter a realm where the desires and burdens of Christ become alive in their spirit, soul, and body. That means they feel the pain of the agony of the Holy Spirit. Therefore, the prayer of an intercessor is called "travailing prayer" or "agonizing prayer."

Casual prayers are done with eloquent words, while intercessory prayer is done with weeping, mourning, agonizing, and travail, as though in a labor room in childbirth. In other words, an intercessor cries over God's children in the same way that Jesus cried over Jerusalem in **Matthew 23:37.**

What prayer and Intercession do is touch the heart of God. Whenever the heart of God is touched His heart is then moved with compassion. When God's heart is moved with compassion, He then moves His hand to heal, save and deliver.

INTERCESSORY PAINS

This is the pain that comes with giving birth.

Jeremiah 4:31, Micah 4:10. In intercession, the intercessor feels the same pain in his or her bowels as though in literal labor. This pain is the pain of the burden of the people of God, which usually comes with screaming, agony, etc. Just as a woman gives birth to a child, an intercessor gives birth to breakthroughs in the lives of the Saints of God.

GROANING - Groaning in intercession is a deep emotional sound as though in severe pain, grief, or agony. It may happen in silence in your spirit or in a moaning sound **(John 11:33, Rom 8:23; 2Co 5:2, 2Co 5:4; Luke 19:41-44).** This happens when the Holy Spirit lays upon the intercessor's spirit and soul the burden and pain of Jesus concerning His people. The Holy Spirit also uses this method to intercede for us.

WEEPING - Weeping brings great harvest and is one of the expressions of the Holy Spirit in intercession. Whenever the Spirit weeps in us, we are bearing seeds of deliverance, salvation, and breakthrough (Psalms 126:5-6). This weeping is a weeping that comes either in silence or loud as though in great distress.

MOURNING – Intercessors mourn over the people's sins and the proclaimed judgment of God over a nation or people. In the Old Testament, this was done in several ways: loud lamentation, rending the clothes, wearing sackcloth, sprinkling dust or ashes, and sitting in silence. In this modern time, we do not do these things, nevertheless, we mourn in our souls over God's people and the sins of the country.

WAILING – Wailing is making a loud crying noise in intercession. This is the same as howling. However, God uses you, do not be ashamed or embarrassed you are doing the will of God (obedience), and on the job-saving lives!

Okay, let's briefly go over what we have learned.

Deliverance! Is a must; it is key to getting the revelations and downloads on what we need to intercede about. Remember becoming a clean vessel allows God to move freely within us. Never tell God nothing is wrong with you when He tells you there is, always yield to deliverance God works in layers, this is a process, go through the process!

Development! Developing a consecrated lifestyle, becoming one with our Father, building a relationship with Him, and consuming the word of God will begin to open the areas in your life that God has destined for you! It will also open who you are and who God created you to be, Holy Spirit will be able to teach and navigate through this process.

Deployment! Remember the commandments, and stick to them! Always remember to be led by the Holy Spirit, without Him we sound like a clinging symbol. Don't be afraid to step out and be different, be who God created you to be! Dive into the deep and become so saturated that you may be able to produce what God's word was sent out to do! Always remember that you have people across the world standing with you in intercession, you are not alone, be bold and courageous in the Lord!

ALRIGHT, INTERCESSORS LET'S GO!

NOTES

CHAPTER 5
A SPECIAL PRAYER
For the Start of Your Journey

Then the king said to the man of God, "Intercede with the LORD your God and pray for me that my hand may be restored." So the man of God interceded with the LORD, and the king's hand was restored and became as it was before.
1 Kings 13:6. 6

Dear Heavenly Father,

I lift every person that has read this book. I pray that they will have divine visitation from you. I pray that every heart is healed, set free and delivered. They will begin to know you on another level, they will become your heartbeat. I unlock their five senses and thrust them forward into their next level of Intercession. I speak that they will launch themselves out into deep waters and submerge themselves. The deeper they go, the more purified they will become. Father set their hearts on fire. STIR THEM UP! Allow their prophetic wells to erupt and the sounds of Heaven begin to rest in their ear gates. God let them have a love that is so pure that no enemy in hell can stand against it.

Every assignment you give to them I speak your manifestations and they will be able to be witnesses of how great you are. I prophesy they will be like trees planted by the waters that sends out its roots by the stream. It does not fear when heat comes, its leaves are always green. It has no worries in the year of drought or never fails to bear fruit. I prophecy that they will not have to muster courage and strength on their own, they will simply submit to the spirit of God that is within them. For I am convinced that neither death nor life, neither angels nor demons, neither the present nor the future, nor any powers, neither height nor depth, nor anything else in all creation, will be able to separate them from the love of God that is in Christ Jesus, our Lord.

May God's blessings and favor be upon you all.

PROPHET GAIL HURT

Is a loving mother who entered her God ordained calling as a Prophetic Intercessor in 2012. Her mission is to pursue and walk in the purpose of God. She desires to Leave No Man Left Behind through teaching, coaching, engaging, and encouraging others to believe in the possibilities. While focusing on all ages of women who have lost their way, Prophet Gail Hurt rejuvenates and restores them back to life with a foundation rooted and grounded in Christ Jesus.

A NOTE FROM THE AUTHOR

I encourage you to go out and purchase the Heart of An Intercessor Training Manual and A More Excellent Way to Cover Your Leader in Prayer book and manual by Prophet Renee Jacob.

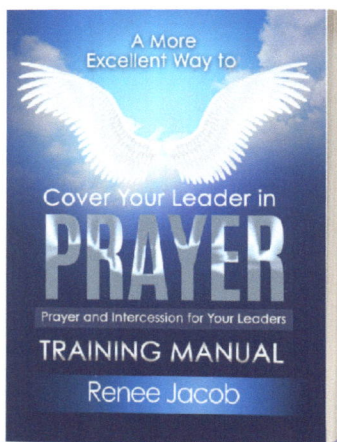

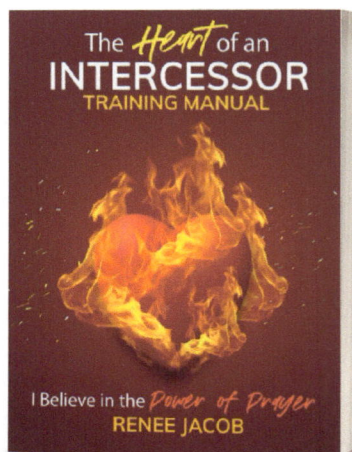

She has a heart that flows with love and compassion that empowers her to intercede with great power and authority to manifest breakthroughs. Prophet Renee is the overseer of Impact for Change Ministries, the host of the radio broadcast Advancing the Kingdom and the host of a TV broadcast on CFAN.

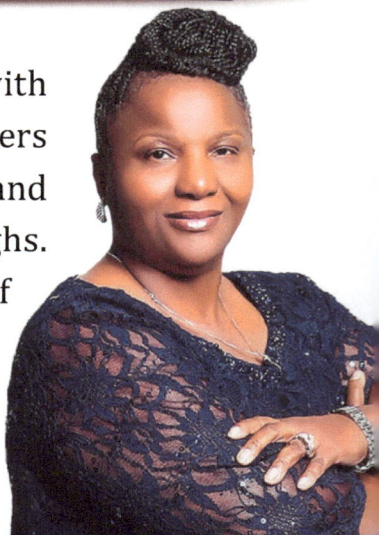

NOTES

NOTES

NOTES

NOTES